Raspberry Pi GPS using Python 2.7 or 3.4
For Raspbian Jessie Linux using GPSD gps3
Python language, runs on most operating systems

Herb Norbom
Author of:
Raspberry Pi Python Projects Python3 and Tkinter/Ttk
Python3.3.4 Tkinter/Ttk Widgets and Sqlite3
Raspberry Pi GPS using Python For Windows and Debian-Linux
Raspberry Pi Camera Controls For Windows and Debian-Linux using Python 3.2
Raspberry Pi Camera Controls For Windows and Debian-Linux using Python 2.7
Raspberry Pi Robot with Camera and Sound using Python 3.2
Raspberry Pi Robot with Camera and Sound
Robot Wireless Control Made Simple with Python and C
Python Version 2.6 Introduction using IDLE
Python Version 2.7 Introduction using IDLE
Python Version 3.2 Introduction using IDLE and PythonWin
Bootloader Source Code for ATMega168 using STK500 For Microsoft Windows
Bootloader Source Code for ATMega168 using STK500 For Debian-Linux
Bootloader Source Code for ATMega328P using STK500 For Microsoft Windows
Bootloader Source Code for ATMega328P using STK500 For Debian-Linux
Books Available on Amazon and CreateSpace

Where we are aware of a trademark that name has been printed with a Capital Letter.

Great care has been taken to provide accurate information, by both the author and the publisher, no expressed or implied warranty of any kind is given. No liability is assumed for any damages in connection with any information provided.

Table of Contents

FOREWARD..3
PREFACE..3
  Why Python?..3
  Supplies and Devices..4
  Work Directories-Raspberry Pi...5
  Setup Windows PC..5
  Program or Text Editor Notes..5
  Python Start 5
GPS Set Up..7
    Setup USB Adapter..8
    Testing the USB Adapter Cable and GPS..9
    Install gps3..13
Pythagorean Theorem...15
    Pythagorean Python Program...16
Latitude and Longitude...18
    The graticule on the sphere..18
Haversine Formula..19
    Haversine Python Program...21
Script for Starting GPS...23
GPS Python Program Discussion..24
    What our GPS program looks like..27
    Satellite Information...29
gpsUSBPython2and3.py PROGRAM...30
THE END OR THE BEGINNING...42
APPENDIX...42
  Hardware and Operating Systems used...42
  Summary for Raspberry Pi Setup..42
  VNC install on Windows 10...43
  logging on to the Pi from Windows Direct Connection via Ether-Net................................44
  logging on to the Pi from Ubuntu-Linux via Router or Wireless..44
  logging on to the Pi from Ubuntu-Linux Direct Connection via Ether-Net........................44
  Battery or Auxiliary Power...47
  PuTTY for Windows...47
  PuTTY for Linux..48
  Geany for Windows..49
  Geany for Raspberry Pi..49
  Linux Shell Scripts...49
  Linux Commands..50
  GPS setup for Travel..52
Reference Sites..53
  Raspberry..53
  Raspberry – GPS..53
  https://www.pinterest.com/kmcdavid/social-studies-latitude-and-longitude/.......................53
  Python..53
  Tkinter..53
  Windows...54
  Linux..54

Direct Connect Ether-net..54
PuTTY...54
Geany..54

FOREWARD

The Raspberry Pi is a wonderful computer that is supported by a growing user base. The Pi's price, low power requirements and small footprint make it very suitable for a variety of applications. As additional hardware is made available I expect the Pi's popularity to continue its strong growth. One of the additions to the Pi accessories is the Pi's GPS. With the Pi's support of WiFi one can quickly visualize many applications.

PREFACE

This book is an updated version of "Raspberry Pi GPS using Python For Windows and Debian-Linux". There have been numerous changes since the original book was published. Python3 is now supported for the Python module gps3. We will need to download the Python module gps3 and the gspd components. The newer versions of Raspbian include the VNC server software. This makes running the Raspberry headless much easier.

The book includes what we need to operate the GPS from a remote PC running Windows or Ubuntu-Linux; and for running the GPS from your Pi console. In the Appendix I am going to include information on how to direct connect your Raspberry Pi to a Windows Notebook or Linux PC using a direct ether-net connection. Our GPS control program can run using Python 2.7.9 or Python 3.4 under Linux. At this point the Python gps module is not available for Windows, therefore we will run from the Raspberry and use VNC to view on Windows.

See the Appendix for a summary of the hardware and operating systems used.

For setting up the Raspberry Pi I provide a summary in the Appendix. There are excellent sources on line, no use building a new wheel. I suggest you get the biggest SD card you can. The 4 GB will probably be insufficient. I recommend you have several SD cards (minimum size 8Gb) and learn how to back your system up.

While we are going to setup the Raspberry Pi to be operational without a monitor, keyboard or mouse I suggest that as you are learning and testing that you leave those items connected.

These programs are designed for a full screen monitor, if you desire to make the Raspberry Pi very portable consider the small displays and keyboards that are available and modify the code as needed. As I plan to run the device remotely I have provided for battery power, see the Appendix.

Why Python?

Even If you have never programmed before, I suggest you start with Python. We are going to be using a lot of Python. Everyone has their own favorite programming language and good reasons for it. My choice is Python. There are several reasons for choosing Python, they include:
- Object Oriented – will flow with events rather than straight lines
- Not compiled, uses an interpreter – therefore, quick results while developing applications
- Runs on Windows, Linux, Unix, even Apple – it is portable
- There is lot of FREE information on the web about it
- Python is free and already installed on your Raspberry Pi
- There are a lot of free modules - you may need to enhance your project

- What you learn, program flow and structure will to some extent carry over to C, C++ or C#, or whatever language you evolve to
- Python has a good built-in GUI, Tkinter

Just because Python uses an interpreter do not think you are limited in terms of program size and complexity.

Raspbian version 8 (Jessie) has multiple versions of Python installed. As of this time Python 2.7.9 is the default version but Python 3.4.2 is also installed. If you are not familiar with Python at all consider the book 'Python Version 2.7 or 3.2 Introduction using IDLE' and Python 3.3.4 Tkinter/Ttk Widgets and Sqlite3 all sold on Amazon, yes I am the author, sorry about the self promoting. This book includes the complete printed source code. The electronic or digitized code is available for an additional fee and for a limited time, see http://www.rymax.biz/. If you are interested you can search Amazon using my name for a complete list of books.

Supplies and Devices

- Of course you need the Raspberry Pi and various hardware items listed under Supplies and Devices. You will need to get the Pi working over a wireless or ether-net connection. The internet connection is needed for various modules that need to be downloaded.

- You are going to be downloading software, if you do not have a high speed connection this is going to be very difficult.

- You need to setup your directories, just makes life easier.

- We will write our Programs using Python as that is installed on the Raspberry Pi and it is an excellent choice anyway. The programs will run under Python2 or Python3

The following parts list can be viewed as a starting point, substitute as you like. The Raspberry Pi 3 is sold by a number of distributors. The Raspberry Pi Model B should work as well as the newer Raspberry Pi Zero W. Prices shown are subject to change.

Part	Possible Source	Source Part #	Approx. Price
Raspberry Pi 3 Model B with 1 G of ram	adafruit	ID: 3055	39.95
Raspberry Pi GPS	adafruit	ID: 746	39.95
GPS Antenna -External	adafruit	ID: 960 (OPTIONAL)	12.95
SMA to uFL Adapter Cable	adafruit	ID: 851 (OPTIONAL)	3.95
USB to TTL Serial Cable	adafruit	ID: 954	9.95
Power supply	adafruit	Check for one working with Raspberry	
SD Memory Card(min8GB)	adafruit	many choices available	
SD Card Reader/Writer	Find best one	your PC may have one	

I did not include a monitor, keyboard, mouse or ether-net cable, hopefully you have spares to use while you get everything running; it is possible to run the Pi without them. (Note, a standard ether-net cable will work.) For the Raspberry items in particular check out the package deals that are available. While I have used these suppliers I am not saying they are the best or the least expensive. I am not affiliated with any of them.

Work Directories-Raspberry Pi

We are going to be writing a number of programs and it can get very confusing where they are located. Also from a backup view point it is nice to have them in a separate directory. I suggest you make a separate directory now. I called my directory 'GPSbook' in the Pi home directory.

Setup Windows PC

For our remote control we are going to need some software on the PC. There are a number of options but I am just going to list what I was able to get working. You may want or need PuTTY. PuTTY provides a communication link for our PC, just nice to have (see Appendix). We will use the VNC viewer and the enabled VNC on the Raspberry. For installing VNC Viewer on your PC see the appendix. For remote viewing we 'boot' our Raspberry Pi and then from our Windows PC log on to the Raspberry Pi. If you are connecting via a router connection this is pretty straight forward. With everything working we will log on to the Raspberry Pi using "pi".

Program or Text Editor Notes

I am going to use Geany on my Raspberry Pi as it is pretty good and is already installed with the Raspbian Jessie OS. You can use any text editor (nano, vi or vim or whatever you like). Each has pluses and minuses. One of the nice features of Geany is that you can run the program right from Geany. Once you are running the program remotely or as they say 'headless' with no monitor attached you may appreciate this feature. See the Appendix for setting the version of Python you which to run with Geany.

In the programs you may note that I use "tabs" vs spaces for indenting. My tab is set for 5 spaces. I have found this makes the programs a little easier to read. You may also notice in the printed source code that some lines are continued on multiple lines. Generally Python code can be split to a separate line on a ",". A continuation character of "\" can also be used.

Python Start

The following walks you through your first Python program.

Test your Python and Python3. For Python 2.7.9 type 'python' at the prompt. You should get a message from Python. Mine says Python 2.7.9 (default, Sep 17, 2016....) and gives the Python prompt of >>>.

For Python 3.4.2 type 'python3' at the # prompt. If all is well you should get a message from Python. Mine says Python 3.4.2 (default, Oct 19, 2014....) and gives the Python prompt of >>>.

To exit the Python prompt you can enter "Crtl z"; or "Ctrl-d" returns to your command prompt.

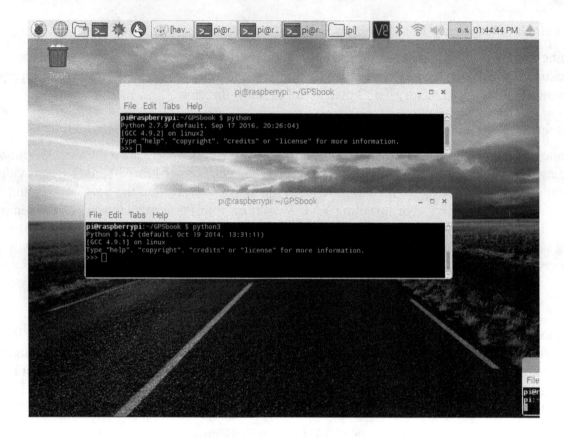

I have logged onto the Raspberry Pi from my Windows PC using VNC, log-in as pi. Or run from the console GUI. I suggest you change to our GPSbook directory.

I have written the programs to use Python 2.7.9 or Python 3.4.2. I like to run from the command line, as you will see in the exhibits.

Enter the program code using Geany and save file as 'simpleTest.py'. The 'py' extension is required by Python, Geany also uses it to identify the script or program type and to give some helpful hints.

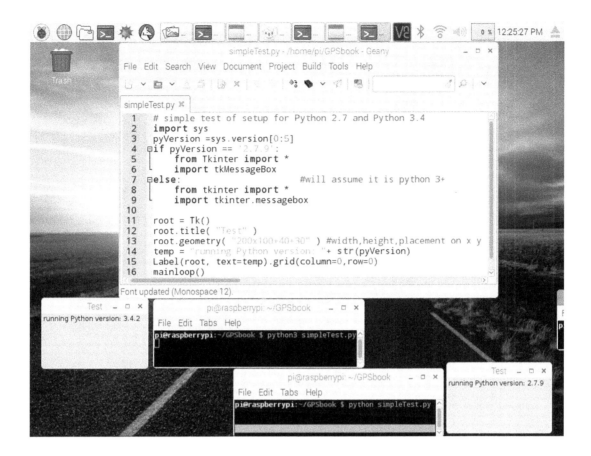

As you can see even at this level there is a little difference in the code. The output is the same.

I am sure you are aware, but just in case I need to mention how to shutdown your Pi. You should always run a 'shutdown' procedure. These procedures ensure an orderly closing of files and help prevent corruption of your SD. From the command line you can run "shutdown -h now", if not logged in with sufficient permissions, precede the command with "sudo". On the Pi Desktop GUI there is a shutdown item on the menu.

GPS Set Up

There are excellent references on line for setting the GPS up. I am not going to go into great depth on the setup. Basic instructions, reference sites and insight as to some of the problems I had are provided. A very good site to start with is from Adafruit. As this is where I purchased my GPS from it is relevant.

http://learn.adafruit.com/adafruit-ultimate-gps-on-the-raspberry-pi?view=all

Assuming you purchased the USB to TTL serial cable the following applies.

The GPS comes with breakaway header pins that you need to solder to your GPS. Note in the picture the External Antenna and USB TTL adapter cable are shown.

Connect the GPS and USB TTL cable.

RED wire to VIN,
BLACK wire to GND,
GREEN wire to RX
and WHITE wire to TX

Plug the TTL Cable into Raspberry USB port.

Setup USB Adapter

After plugging in the adapter we need to determine to see where the device is connected to. From the command prompt enter   ls /dev/ttyUSB*

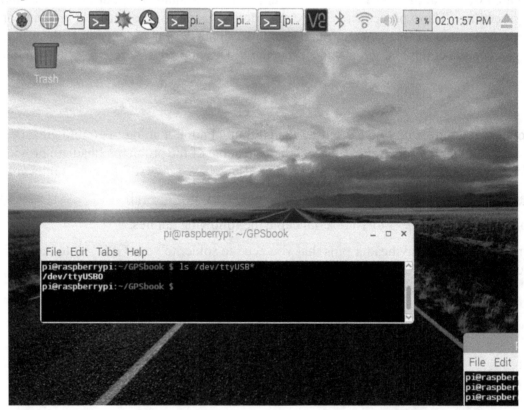

To get additional information on the adapter enter   sudo lsusb   You should see the "Prolific Technology Inc" device.

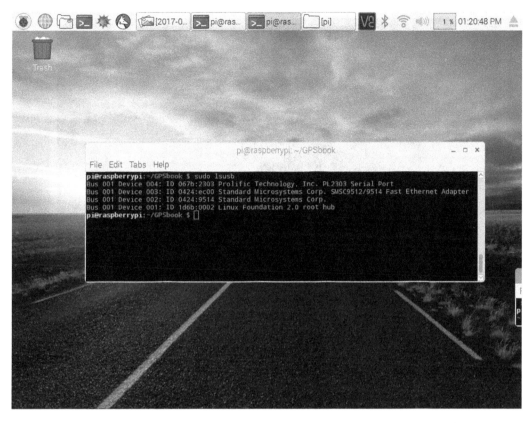

Testing the USB Adapter Cable and GPS

To see if you are getting a signal enter 'cat /dev/ttyUSB0', if you are connected should get something similar to the following illustration. (If not running try using sudo.)   To stop enter Ctrl + c or Ctrl + z.

This is the raw data, to be of use it will need to be parsed. Lucky that has been done for us as shown later.

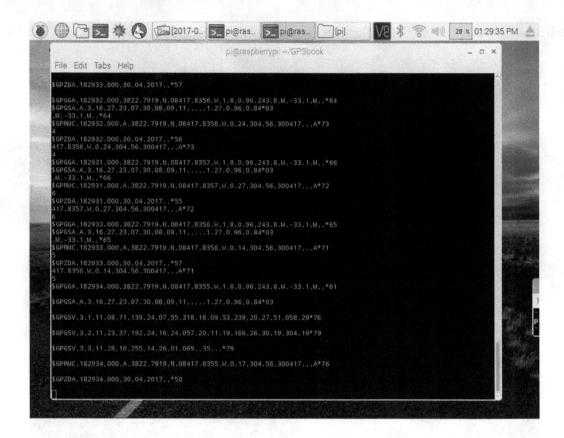

We need to download software to process the raw data for our future programs. From the console type:

'sudo apt-get install gpsd gpsd-clients python-gps '(Note three applications). You should get display similar to the following.

After the install is finished issue a couple of commands, if running Raspbian Jessie.

For Raspbian Jessie we need a systemd service fix. What we just installed by default listens on a local socket, we need to stop it. Enter the following at the console.
  "sudo systemctl stop gpsd.socket
  "sudo systemctl disable gpsd.socket

If for some reason you want to enable the default gpsd systemd service run the following.
  "sudo systemctl enable gpsd.socket
  "sudo systemctl start gpsd.socket

(A good idea is to wait until the GPS gets a 'FIX' on satellite, the flashing LED slows to approximately every 20 seconds. The GPS can take some time to obtain a FIX, approximately 30 seconds to a couple of minutes.)

To run gpsd manually enter "sudo gpsd /dev/ttyUSB0 -F /var/run/gpsd.sock"

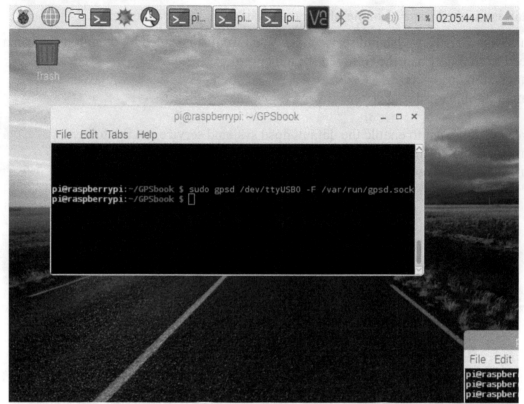

To see our data from the GPS parsed and displayed enter the following from the command line.

'cgps -s'

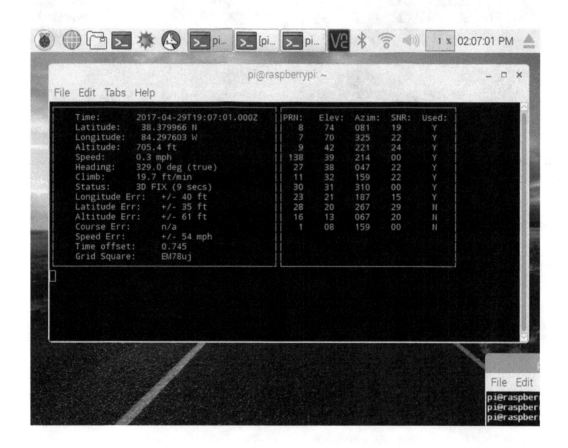

The display should keep running until you end it.

To stop enter Ctrl + c or Ctrl + z.

If the above starts and abruptly ends chances are that the gps device is not getting a strong enough signal. Try using the antenna and or moving to a window. If that does not help try stopping the gpsd and restarting. To stop "sudo killall gpsd". In the following exhibit you will see I ran the command twice to be certain the process stopped.

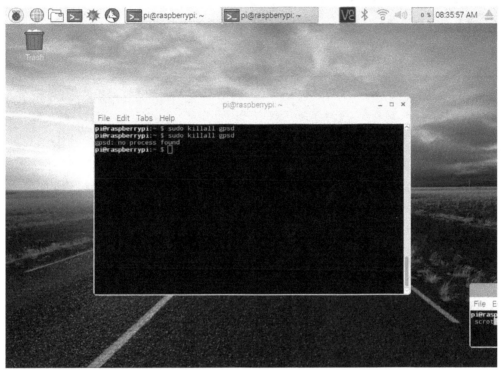

Install gps3

This is the Python module we need for our program to interpret the raw data. You will only need to install for the version of Python you plan to use but if you have room nice to have it installed under both Python versions.

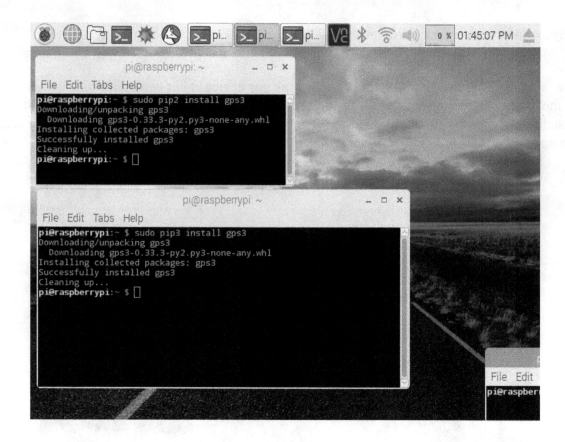

We need to issue a command to start the processing of the GPS output. (A good idea is to wait until the GPS gets a 'FIX' on satellite, the flashing LED slows to approximately every 20 seconds. The GPS can take some time to obtain a FIX, approximately 30 seconds to a couple of minutes.) Enter at the command prompt 'sudo gpsd /dev/ttyUSB0 -F /var/run/gpsd.sock'. (If not previously done)

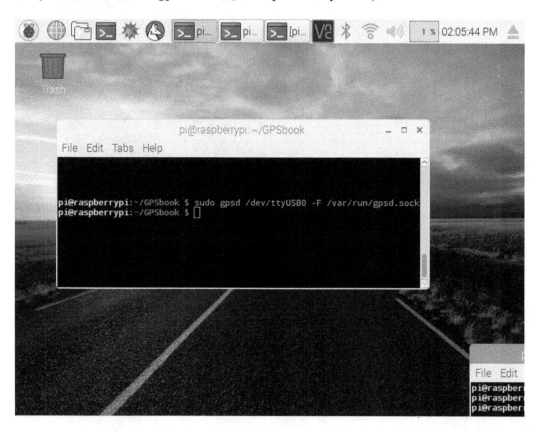

Pythagorean Theorem

We are going to use our GPS for determining our location and for calculating distance to other GPS coordinates. To get our heads into gear I want to start with a simple program for calculating distance for the hypotenuse of a right triangle. The formula is $a^2 + b^2 = c^2$, with c being the hypotenuse.

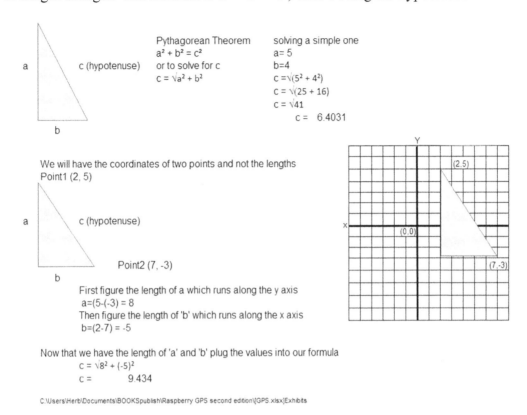

C:\Users\Herb\Documents\BOOKSpublish\Raspberry GPS second edition\[GPS.xlsx]Exhibits

While we are going to be working with more complex numbers our formula will remain basically the same. Until we get into large distances and want to account for the shape of the earth, more on that later. To get started a simple Python program for the computation has been prepared.

The output is the same for both versions as shown in the following.

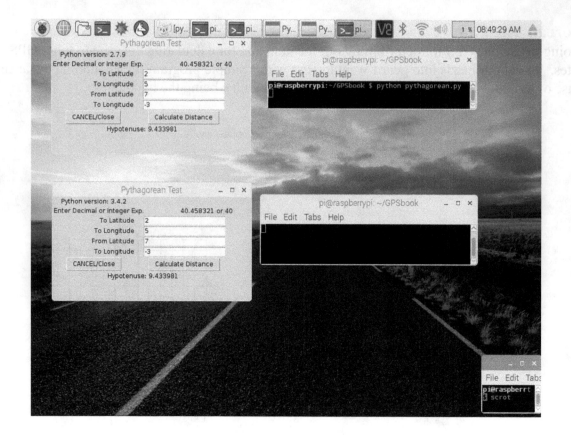

Pythagorean Python Program

```
# Pythagorean test python 2.7.9 or 3.4.2
import sys
class SELF:
        pass                   # define later as needed


SELF.pyVersion =sys.version[0:5]
if SELF.pyVersion == '2.7.9':
        from Tkinter import *
        import tkMessageBox
else:                                   #will assume it is python 3+
        from tkinter import *
        import tkinter.messagebox


from math import sqrt


def distance():
     try:
             lat1 = float(SELF.Lat1.get())
             lon1 = float(SELF.Lon1.get())
             lat2 = float(SELF.Lat2.get())
```

```python
                lon2 = float(SELF.Lon2.get())
        except:
                if SELF.pyVersion == '2.7.9':
                        tkMessageBox.showerror("ERROR", "Enter decimal or integer")
                        return
                else:
                        tkinter.messagebox.showerror("ERROR", "Enter decimal or integer")
                        return


        dlat =  lat1 -lat2          # distance between x points
        dlon = lon1 - lon2          # distance between y points

        d1 = dlat*dlat + dlon*dlon       #square the distances and add together
        d = sqrt(d1)                     # square root to get the Hypotenuse
        temp = "Hypotenuse: "+ str('{:,.6f}'.format(d))
        Label(SELF.root,text = temp).grid(column=0,columnspan=2,row= 10)

def setup():
        SELF.root = Tk()
        SELF.root.title( "Pythagorean Test" )
        SELF.root.geometry( "400x200+40+30" ) #width,height,placement on x y axis
        temp = "Python version: "+ str(SELF.pyVersion)
        Label(SELF.root, text=temp).grid(column=0,row=0)

        Label(SELF.root,text='Enter Decimal or Integer Exp. \
                40.458321 or 40').grid(column=0,columnspan=2,row=1)

        Label(SELF.root,text="To Latitude").grid(column=0, row=3,sticky=(E))
        SELF.Lat1=DoubleVar()
        e2=Entry(SELF.root, textvariable=SELF.Lat1)
        e2.grid(column=1, row=3)
        e2.delete(0,END)
        e2.focus()

        Label(SELF.root,text="To Longitude").grid(column=0, row=4,sticky=(E))
        SELF.Lon1=DoubleVar()
        e3=Entry(SELF.root, textvariable=SELF.Lon1)
        e3.grid(column=1, row=4)
        e3.delete(0,END)

        Label(SELF.root,text="From Latitude").grid(column=0, row=6,sticky=(E))
        SELF.Lat2=DoubleVar()
```

```
e2=Entry(SELF.root, textvariable=SELF.Lat2)
e2.grid(column=1, row=6)
e2.delete(0,END)
e2.focus()

Label(SELF.root,text="To Longitude").grid(column=0, row=7,sticky=(E))
SELF.Lon2=DoubleVar()
e3=Entry(SELF.root, textvariable=SELF.Lon2)
e3.grid(column=1, row=7)
e3.delete(0,END)

Button(SELF.root, text="CANCEL/Close",
        command=SELF.root.destroy).grid(column=0, row=9)
Button(SELF.root, text="Calculate Distance",
        command=distance).grid(column=1, row=9)

if __name__=='__main__':
    setup()
    mainloop()
```

Latitude and Longitude

The following are from Wikipedia.org https://en.wikipedia.org/wiki/Latitude and
https://upload.wikimedia.org/wikipedia/commons/5/53/MercNormSph_enhanced.png

The graticule on the sphere

The graticule is formed by the lines of constant latitude and constant longitude, which are constructed with reference to the rotation axis of the Earth. The primary reference points are the poles where the axis of rotation of the Earth intersects the reference surface. Planes which contain the rotation axis intersect the surface at the meridians; and the angle between any one meridian plane and that through Greenwich (the Prime Meridian) defines the longitude: meridians are lines of constant longitude. The plane through the centre of the Earth and perpendicular to the rotation axis intersects the surface at a great circle called the Equator. Planes parallel to the equatorial plane intersect the surface in circles of constant latitude; these are the parallels. The Equator has a latitude of 0°, the North Pole has a latitude of 90° North (written 90° N or +90°), and the South Pole has a latitude of 90° South (written 90° S or −90°). The latitude of an arbitrary point is the angle between the equatorial plane and the radius to that point.

The latitude, as defined in this way for the sphere, is often termed the spherical latitude, to avoid ambiguity with auxiliary latitudes defined in subsequent sections of this article.

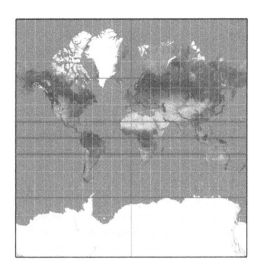

Haversine Formula

We have graduated to working with the Haversine Formula. A good reference site is:
http://en.wikipedia.org/wiki/Haversine_formula . The formula looks intimidating, but if we approach in small steps it becomes somewhat easy to solve. Luckily you do not need to have a solid foundation in trigonometry to program the function. Python has the functions for sin, cos, etc built in just like the square root that we used earlier. As this formula takes into account the earth as a sphere we begin to work with radians. There are a lot of web sites that can give you better insight as to 'the why', so I leave those types of explanations to them. As you are doing the calculations you will probably want to check your computations. A great way to do that is by going to various web sites. You are going to find differences in distances; part of the reason is the sites may use a different earth radius. The earth is not a perfect sphere, more of a pear. For the purpose here we will be close enough.

	A	B	C	D	E	F	G
1	Haversine Formula			Good Reference Site:		http://en.wikipedia.org/wiki/Haversine_formula	
2	Distance= $2*R * ASIN(\sqrt{[SIN^2((Lat1-Lat2)/2)+COS(Lat1) * COS(Lat2) * SIN^2((Lon1-Lon2)/2)]}$						
3	'R' for the earth Radius = 6371			We also need to keep in mind that we will be working in radians			
4		Coordinates to work with for testing					
5		Lat1 =	33.58000	Lon1 =	-85.85000		
6		Lat2 =	49.02211	Lon2 =	2.54162		
7	**STEP1**						
8	We need to calculate the difference for Lat and Lon, convert to radians and divide by 2						using Excel Formulas
9	change in Latitude in radians divided by 2 =			dLat =	-0.134757831		=Radians((C5-C6)/2)
10	change in Longitude in radians divided by 2 =			dLon =	-0.7713624		=Radians((E5-E6)/2)
11	change just Lat1 into Radians =			rLat1 =	0.586081563		=Radians(C5)
12	change just Lat2 into Radians =			rLat2 =	0.855597226		=Radians(C6)
13							
14	**STEP2**	Plug in all calculations under the square root sign, set that equal to STEP2					
15	Calculate sin of dLat =	sdLat =	-0.13435034				=SIN(F9)
16	Calculate cos of rLat1=	crLat1 =	0.83311436				=COS(F11)
17	Calculate cos of rLat2=	crLat2 =	0.65576774				=COS(F12)
18	Calculate sin of dLon=	sdLon =	-0.69711267				=SIN(F10)
19	STEP2 = sdLat * sdLat + (crLat1 * crLat2 * sdLon * sdLon))=				0.283547632		=+(D15*D15)+(D16*D17*D18*D18)
20							
21	**STEP3**	Take the square root of STEP2					
22	STEP3 = sqrt(STEP2) =		0.53249191				=SQRT(F19)
23							
24	**STEP4**	Compute the ArcSin of STEP3					
25	STEP4 = asin(STEP3) =		0.56154185				=ASIN(D22)
26							
27	**STEP5**	Multiply STEP4 by 2 and by the Earth Radius(R)					
28	distance = STEP4 * 2 * R =		**7,155.17**	km			=+D25 * 2 * 6371

With our math working I put the same logic into the Python programs. When we get to writing our main program we will combine steps. It is a lot easier for me to understand when taken in steps. I have tried to use the same names and flow as in the preceding spreadsheet Illustration. I used a slightly different radius in the following example.

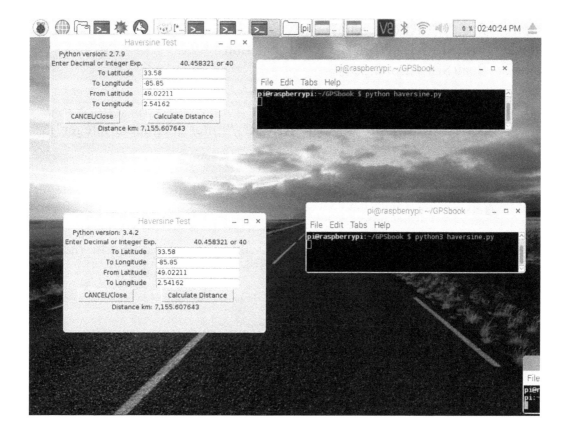

Haversine Python Program

```
#!/usr/bin/env python
# Haversine formula example in Python
# Author: Wayne Dyck modified Herb Norbom

import sys
class SELF:
        pass                    # define later as needed

SELF.pyVersion =sys.version[0:5]
if SELF.pyVersion == '2.7.9':
        from Tkinter import *
        import tkMessageBox
else:                                   #will assume it is python 3+
        from tkinter import *
        import tkinter.messagebox



import math

def distance():
        try:
                lat1 = float(SELF.Lat1.get())        #origin
```

```python
            lon1 = float(SELF.Lon1.get())
            lat2 = float(SELF.Lat2.get())        #destination
            lon2 = float(SELF.Lon2.get())
        except:
            if SELF.pyVersion == '2.7.9':
                tkMessageBox.showerror("ERROR", "Enter decimal or integer")
                return
            else:
                tkinter.messagebox.showerror("ERROR", "Enter decimal or integer")
                return


        radius = 6371.393 #km     mi=3,959 https://en.wikipedia.org/wiki/Earth_radius
#STEP1
        dlat = math.radians(lat2-lat1)
        dlon = math.radians(lon2-lon1)
#STEP2
        a = math.sin(dlat/2) * math.sin(dlat/2) + math.cos(math.radians(lat1)) \
            * math.cos(math.radians(lat2)) * math.sin(dlon/2) * math.sin(dlon/2)
#STEP3
        c = 2 * math.asin(math.sqrt(a))
#STEP4
        d = radius * c
        temp = "Distance km: "+ str('{:,.6f}'.format(d))
        Label(SELF.root,text = temp).grid(column=0,columnspan=2,row= 10)



def setup():
        SELF.root = Tk()
        SELF.root.title( "Haversine Test" )
        SELF.root.geometry( "400x200+40+30" ) #width,height,placement on x y axis
        temp = "Python version: "+ str(SELF.pyVersion)
        Label(SELF.root, text=temp).grid(column=0,row=0)

        Label(SELF.root,text='Enter Decimal or Integer Exp. \
            40.458321 or 40').grid(column=0,columnspan=2,row=1)

        Label(SELF.root,text="To Latitude").grid(column=0, row=3,sticky=(E))
        SELF.Lat1=DoubleVar()
        e2=Entry(SELF.root, textvariable=SELF.Lat1)
        e2.grid(column=1, row=3)
        e2.delete(0,END)
        e2.focus()

        Label(SELF.root,text="To Longitude").grid(column=0, row=4,sticky=(E))
        SELF.Lon1=DoubleVar()
```

```
e3=Entry(SELF.root, textvariable=SELF.Lon1)
e3.grid(column=1, row=4)
e3.delete(0,END)

Label(SELF.root,text="From Latitude").grid(column=0, row=6,sticky=(E))
SELF.Lat2=DoubleVar()
e2=Entry(SELF.root, textvariable=SELF.Lat2)
e2.grid(column=1, row=6)
e2.delete(0,END)
e2.focus()

Label(SELF.root,text="To Longitude").grid(column=0, row=7,sticky=(E))
SELF.Lon2=DoubleVar()
e3=Entry(SELF.root, textvariable=SELF.Lon2)
e3.grid(column=1, row=7)
e3.delete(0,END)

Button(SELF.root, text="CANCEL/Close",
        command=SELF.root.destroy).grid(column=0, row=9)
Button(SELF.root, text="Calculate Distance",
        command=distance).grid(column=1, row=9)

if __name__=='__main__':
    setup()
    mainloop()
```

These are some of the sites that I have used to check my calculations:

http://www.movable-type.co.uk/scripts/latlong.html

http://www.gpsvisualizer.com/calculators

Script for Starting GPS

In the following we will setup a script that we can use for starting our GPS. The script includes the command to stop the GPS service before starting it, (commented out). I found this to be helpful, in particular while getting everything running. While a message is generated if the GPS service is not running, the error is benign. I saved the script in the same directory as our programs. Once you write the script you need to make it executable, see the Appendix if not sure how to do that. When you first power up the GPS you will probably see the red LED flashing fairly rapidly. While getting a satellite fix the LED flashes rapidly. The LED flashes approximately every 20 seconds when a fix is obtained. Once you have a fix you can execute the script. Took me awhile to catch on to that, even though I am sure it is mentioned somewhere. If you don't wait you will probably have some problems with the displays.

```
# !/bin/bash
# script for starting GPS service, run as sudo
#sometimes need to run 'killall gpsd' twice to clean out old
```

```
echo "running StartGPS script"
#'killall' will print 'no process found if nothing running'
#killall gpsd  #if running this from command line use sudo
#this start the gps #if running this from command line use sudo
gpsd /dev/ttyUSB0 -F /var/run/gpsd.sock
#echo "test by running cgps -s" # this does not need sudo
```

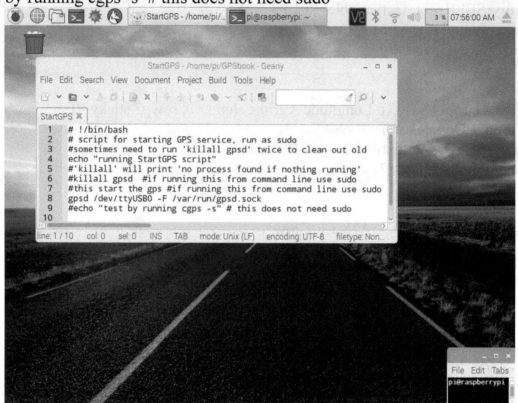

You can test the script by typing at the prompt where the script is saved:

sudo ./StartGPS

   Notice the './' between sudo and Start.

Depending on where you have saved the file you may need to precede sudo with the path as shown below.

/usr/bin/sudo ./StartGPS

GPS Python Program Discussion

The program is designed to run under Python 2.7.9 or Python 3.4.2 +

The program uses the gps3 0.33.3 module. This is a different interface than I used in my first GPS book. One of the many nice things is that it can run under both versions of Python.

class DISP and SELF

The first classes I want to setup are for receiving and processing the GPS information. We set up two instances of the class (SELF and DISP) to enable an efficient display and update of our GPS data. The other ways I have tried to do this have resulted in a very noticeable flicker, virtually gone with this method. The default values that are assigned are just to help visualize while the data is initially processed.

List data class for my Locations

This list is used to store location names and coordinates. I plan to plot and add locations around my property to give my robot an idea of where it is in reference to the property. Here I went ahead and added some airport locations. Of course change this however you like. For Geocaching I am planning on adding locations and one of the small displays to travel with. (I do not have what I want to use for a small display at this point, the small package to travel with will be a future enhancement.) But I do show in the Appendix how to direct connect to your Windows or Ubuntu-Linux Laptop for a little portability.

myGPSdisplay

This is where our current GPS data is displayed. I use a thread timer to update the data (msgFromGPS). Works pretty good, at least no noticeable flicker. I am sure you will note the StringVar(), this is needed to get the updated data to display.

def displayDistance

With this display I was not concerned with a flicker as you need to press the Calculate Distance button to update the data. I went ahead and did the calculations for converting km to miles and m to feet for those of us not used to one or the other.

def runningGPS

This function retrieves the GPS parsed data. I do just a little bit of rounding to make the display more consistent. As you are running your GPS you probably have noticed that even while standing still you get a reading for speed, even your latitude and longitude jump around a bit. The rounding is intended to reduce the small fluctuations, hopefully without hurting accuracy. I put the entire process in an error catching routine. I also wanted to be able to display some additional information, errors, direction, etc. The additional values are not always present so I but them in an additional error catching routine, but it just gives a free pass if caught.

def calDist

Most of the code is just to line up the 'To' and 'From' coordinates. I used the 'if' and 'elif' statements as I thought it was pretty easy to follow. On the 'From' side the GPS current position is the number zero position. As you go down through the coding you will see when the 'To' code is 99 we will use your input coordinates.

Once we have determined the "To and From" coordinates we use the Haversine Formula for calculating the distance. This follows what we covered earlier, but a number of steps have been combined.

def customCoord

This function is called when you press the "Custom To Coord" button. A separate window is opened where you can enter coordinates for calculating distance from your current GPS position to what you enter. Enter the coordinates as decimal or integer. Error trapping will ensure that you have entered a decimal or integer when you select the "Calculate Distance" button.

def calCustDist

This function is called when you enter custom coordinates and click the "Calculate Distance" button. This is where the error trapping for decimal format occurs. The coordinates are stored and the 'calDist' function is called to process the calculation.

def buttonSection

I have added a Frame to keep our Buttons organized. The Buttons are standard buttons, you click them and they call a function and run accordingly.

def radioButton

This section contains two frames for holding our Radiobuttons for selecting "To" and "From" locations. Radiobuttons are nice because you can only select one option at a time from the group. With tkinter a tremendous amount of setup is done for you. Radiobuttons are a little bit of a pain because they seem to work best, at least for me, when I used the "IntVar()" to set them up. In my case, I then made that variable global via "SELF Class"so I could access the variable in other functions.

def callStartGPS

This is a short section to stop the gps data display. This does not stop the gpsd. You will need to run "sudo killall gpsd" to accomplish that.

def setupGPS

This procedure defines the local host port and setups up the data stream from the GPS. I have the error trapping routine here because if the GPS is not streaming to the port you will get an error.

The function calls the script we wrote earlier. I found using the complete path names works best. I used the script because I wanted to start the GPS from the program. I put in a sleep command to give a pause; you may want to play with that timing if having problems. Then the procedure for setting up the GPS port is called. For this to work your GPS needs to have acquired satellite Fix, so wait for the GPS LED flash rate to slow down.

def displayUpdating

This function is called by our thread. We need the 'while True' to keep it running as long as the program runs. The function updates our display of GPS data; the 'sleep' gives a slight pause between updates. This is updating on pretty much the same schedule as set for reading the GPS data shown in the next function.

def myTimer

This function is called by our thread. We need the 'while True' to keep it running as long as the program runs. The function reads our GPS data using a call to the function 'runningGPS'. The 'sleep' gives a slight pause between reads. This is updating on pretty much the same schedule as set for displaying the GPS data shown in the previous function. I have not had a problem with a buffer overflow, if you have a problem you may need to shorten the sleep time. You may notice if you issue a 'killall gpsd' command that GPS data continues to be display for a short period while the buffer is emptied.

def threadstart

This function is called when the program starts to initialize and get the threads running. It is important to set the Daemon to True, otherwise when the program ends the threads may continue to run. I have included the error catching as a convenience, but it may be just as good to have the program crash if the threads cannot be started. (Who said that?) The threads are important because they let us maintain control of the program.

def callEXIT

While you can just close the window I have found including an exit routine to be a good practice. Doesn't matter here, but if you are running GPIO items it is good to exit and clean up the GPIO. Just closing the window works fine in this case.

setupTK(frMain)

Because I want this program to run as an import or independently we use the "if __name__ =='__main__':" procedure. If you run the program from a command prompt or directly from Geany the program 'knows' to execute the 'main' and the items below it. If we call the program, after importing it, we will call this function of the program. If you are not familiar with this I hope the fog lifts as you work through the program. When you run from the prompt the program will of course do normal checking and setup. But it will run the function setupTk(1) as its first step. I have set a switch to indicate where the program is being run from, if run independently I want to set up a normal Tk() window, you may think of it as the root or master window. If run or import from a separate program I want to make the window a Toplevel window; as I do not want to have two master or root windows running.

if __name__=='__main__'

When the program is run from the command prompt this is where the program begins running from. The normal behind the scene error checking is of course done. As mentioned above I have set this up so that the program can be imported and called like a function. The first step is to run the named function. The last step of the program is required to get tkinter running that big loop.

What our GPS program looks like

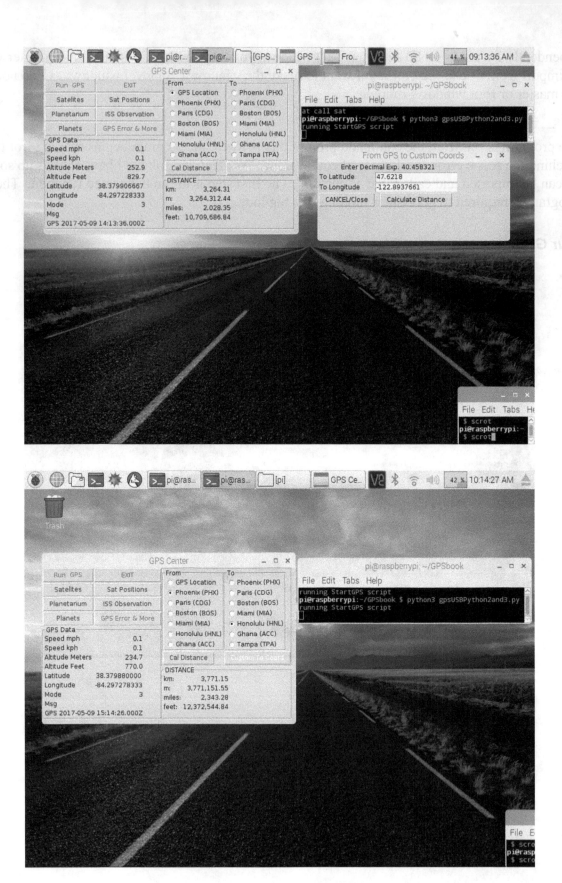

Satellite Information

I thought it useful to be able to display what satellites my system is picking up and using.

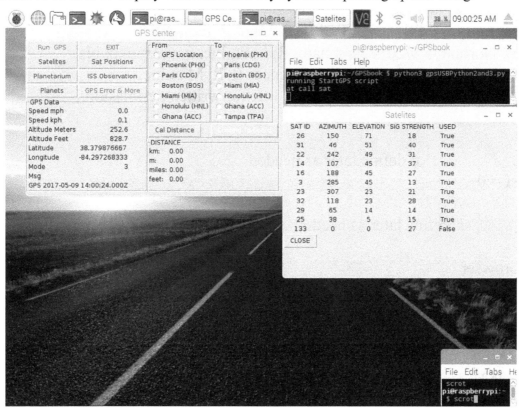

Also as curious I wanted to know where the satellites were positioned.

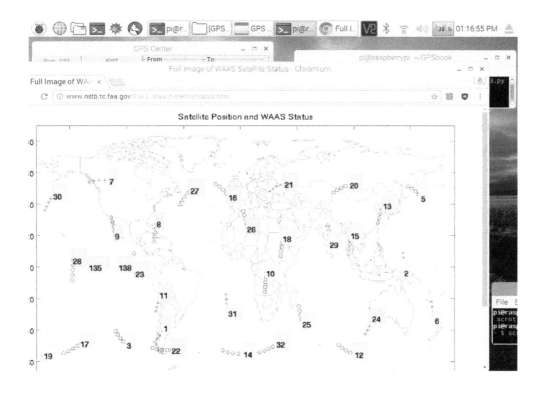

Once I got the web browser working I added a couple more sites that had my interest, Planetarium, ISS Observation and Planets. As I understand the python web browser it calls your default browser.

gpsUSBPython2and3.py PROGRAM

```python
# Control Program for GPS   using Python 2.7.9 or Python 3.4.2
# author Herb Norbom 5/9/2017  company RyMax, Inc. www.rymax.biz
# for personal hobby use only, include references to RyMax Inc.
# Resale or commercial use contact RyMax, Inc. for written permission.


class SELF:
        pass                    # define later as needed
SELF.calDist = 0


class DISP:          # define later as needed
        pass
import webbrowser
import sys
SELF.pyVersion =sys.version[0:5]
if SELF.pyVersion == '2.7.9':
        from Tkinter import *
        import tkMessageBox
else:                                   #will assume it is python 3+
        from tkinter import *
        import tkinter.messagebox


import time
from time import sleep
import threading
from threading import Thread
# for USB connection to GPS
#       You need to have gpsd /dev/ttyUSB0 -F /var/run/gpsd.sock
#       This program runs that in the script  ./StartGPS

from gps3 import agps3
import subprocess
from math import radians, cos, sin, asin, sqrt, atan2



# these are my fixed airport positions.
SELF.rows = []
SELF.rows.append({"Loc":"0","name":"GPS Location",
        "Lat":"0.0", "Lon":"0.0"})
```

```python
SELF.rows.append({"Loc":"1","name":"Phoenix (PHX)",
    "Lat":"33.43406667", "Lon":"-122.0080556"})
SELF.rows.append({"Loc":"2","name":"Paris (CDG)",
    "Lat":"49.022117", "Lon":"2.24162"})
SELF.rows.append({"Loc":"3","name":"Boston (BOS)",
    "Lat":"42.36416677", "Lon":"-70.005"})
SELF.rows.append({"Loc":"4","name":"Miami (MIA)",
    "Lat":"25.79305556", "Lon":"-80.29055556"})
SELF.rows.append({"Loc":"5","name":"Honolulu (HNL)",
    "Lat":"21.3158333", "Lon":"-157.926667"})
SELF.rows.append({"Loc":"6","name":"Ghana (ACC)",
    "Lat":"5.602777778", "Lon":"-0.16805556"})
SELF.rows.append({"Loc":"7","name":"Tampa (TPA)",
    "Lat":"27.9527778", "Lon":"-82.53305556"})


def myGPSdisplay():                          #display messages
    vFrame = LabelFrame(SELF.TOP, width =100, height=100,
    bd=2, text='GPS Data', relief=GROOVE)
    vFrame.grid(column =0,row=1,rowspan=3,sticky=(N,E,S,W))

    DISP.speedMPH = StringVar()
    SELF.speedMPH = 0
    DISP.speedMPH.set(SELF.speedMPH)
    Label(vFrame,textvariable=DISP.speedMPH).grid(column=1,row=2,sticky=(E))
    Label(vFrame,text="Speed mph").grid(column=0,row=2,sticky=(W))

    DISP.speedKPH = StringVar()
    SELF.speedKPH = 0
    DISP.speedKPH.set(SELF.speedKPH)
    Label(vFrame,textvariable=DISP.speedKPH).grid(column=1,row=3,sticky=(E))
    Label(vFrame,text="Speed kph").grid(column=0,row=3,sticky=(W))

    DISP.altM = StringVar()
    SELF.altM = 0
    DISP.altM.set(SELF.altM)
    Label2=Label(vFrame,textvariable=DISP.altM).grid(column=1,row=4,sticky=(E))
    Label(vFrame,text="Altitude Meters").grid(column=0,row=4,sticky=(W))

    DISP.altF = StringVar()
    SELF.altF = 0
    DISP.altF.set(SELF.altF)
    Label2=Label(vFrame,textvariable=DISP.altF).grid(column=1,row=5,sticky=(E))
```

```
        Label(vFrame,text="Altitude Feet").grid(column=0,row=5,sticky=(W))

        DISP.lat = StringVar()
        SELF.lat = 0
        DISP.lat.set(SELF.lat)
        Label(vFrame,textvariable=DISP.lat).grid(column=1,row=6,sticky=(E,W))
        Label(vFrame,text="Latitude").grid(column=0,row=6,sticky=(W))

        DISP.lon = StringVar()
        SELF.lon = 0
        DISP.lon.set(SELF.lon)
        Label(vFrame,textvariable=DISP.lon).grid(column=1,row=7,sticky=(E,W))
        Label(vFrame,text="Longitude").grid(column=0,row=7,sticky=(W))

        DISP.mode = StringVar()
        SELF.mode = 0
        DISP.mode.set(SELF.mode)
        Label(vFrame,textvariable=DISP.mode).grid(column=1,row=8,sticky=(E))
        Label(vFrame,text="Mode").grid(column=0,row=8,sticky=(W))

        DISP.sysMsg = StringVar()
        SELF.sysMsg = "starting"
        DISP.sysMsg.set(SELF.sysMsg)
        Label(vFrame,textvariable=DISP.sysMsg).grid(column=0,columnspan=2,
                row=10,sticky=(E))
        Label(vFrame,text="Msg").grid(column=0,row=9,sticky=(W))

def msgFromGPS():
        speedMPH='{:,.1f}'.format(SELF.speedMPH)
        DISP.speedMPH.set(speedMPH)
        speedKPH='{:,.1f}'.format(SELF.speedKPH)
        DISP.speedKPH.set(speedKPH)
        altM='{:,.1f}'.format(SELF.altM)
        DISP.altM.set(altM)
        altF='{:,.1f}'.format(SELF.altF)
        DISP.altF.set(altF)
        lat='{:.9f}'.format(SELF.lat)
        DISP.lat.set(lat)
        lon='{:.9f}'.format(SELF.lon)
        DISP.lon.set(lon)
        mode='{:}'.format(SELF.mode)
        DISP.mode.set(mode)
```

```python
        DISP.sysMsg.set(SELF.sysMsg)

def displayDistance():
    dFr = LabelFrame(SELF.TOP, width =218, height=218,
    bd=2, text='DISTANCE', relief=GROOVE)
    dFr.grid(column =4,columnspan=2,row=3,sticky=(N,E,S,W))

    Label(dFr,text="km:").grid(column=0,row=0,sticky=(W))
    km='{:,.2f}'.format(SELF.calDist)
    Label(dFr,text=km).grid(column=1,row=0,sticky=(E))

    Label(dFr,text="m:").grid(column=0,row=1,sticky=(W))
    m='{:,.2f}'.format(SELF.calDist*1000)
    Label(dFr,text=m).grid(column=1,row=1,sticky=(E))

    Label(dFr,text="miles:").grid(column=0,row=2,sticky=(W))
    miles='{:,.2f}'.format(SELF.calDist*.621371)
    Label(dFr,text=miles).grid(column=1,row=2,sticky=(E))

    Label(dFr,text="feet:").grid(column=0,row=3,sticky=(W))
    feet='{:,.2f}'.format(SELF.calDist*1000*3.28084)
    Label(dFr,text=feet).grid(column=1,  row=3,sticky=(E))

def runningGPS():
        try:
            for new_data in SELF.gps_socket:
                if SELF.gpsControl.get() == "Run  GPS":
                    if new_data:
            #               print(new_data)         # for debugging if needed
                        SELF.data_stream.unpack(new_data)
                        temp = SELF.data_stream.time
                        DATE = temp[0:10]
                        TIME = temp[11:24]
                        SELF.sysMsg = "GPS "+str(DATE)+" "+str(TIME)
                        tempAltM = SELF.data_stream.alt
                        SELF.altM= round(tempAltM,1)
                        SELF.altF = round(tempAltM * 3.28084,1)
                        SELF.lat= round(SELF.data_stream.lat,9)
                        SELF.lon= round(SELF.data_stream.lon,9)
                        temp = SELF.data_stream.speed
                        SELF.speedKPH = round(temp,1)
                        temp=temp*.621371           #convert kph to mph
```

```python
                SELF.speedMPH = round(temp,1)
                SELF.mode=SELF.data_stream.mode
                try:                # not always present so skip over any error
                        DISP.timeErr.set('{:,.2f}'.format(SELF.data_stream.ept))
                        DISP.LongErr.set('{:,.2f}'.format(SELF.data_stream.epx))
                        DISP.LatErr.set('{:,.2f}'.format(SELF.data_stream.epy))
                        DISP.VertErr.set('{:,.2f}'.format(SELF.data_stream.epv))
                        DISP.climb.set('{:,.2f}'.format(SELF.data_stream.climb))
                        DISP.track.set(SELF.data_stream.track)
                        DISP.DirErr.set(SELF.data_stream.epd)
                        DISP.SpeedErr.set(SELF.data_stream.eps)
                        DISP.ClimbErr.set('{:,.2f}'.format(SELF.data_stream.epc))
                except:
                        pass

        except:
        #       print("At runningGPS Error ,", sys.exc_info()) # for debugging
                SELF.sysMsg = "ERROR running GPS"        # may display several times
                sleep(2)
                SELF.sysMsg = ""


def callSAT():                          #display satellite information
        print("at call sat")
        tempWin= Toplevel()
        tempWin.title("Satelites")
        tempWin.geometry( "470x300+540+30" ) #width, height, placement on x and  y axis
        Label(tempWin,text="SAT ID",width=8).grid(column=0,row=0)
        Label(tempWin,text="AZIMUTH",width=7).grid(column=1,row=0)
        Label(tempWin,text="ELEVATION",width=10).grid(column=2,row=0)
        Label(tempWin,text="SIG STRENGTH",width =11).grid(column=3,row=0)
        Label(tempWin,text="USED",width =6).grid(column=4,row=0)
        Button(tempWin,text="CLOSE",command=tempWin.destroy).grid(column=0,row=14)
        sat = SELF.data_stream.satellites
        tempSize = len(sat)
        try:
                for i in range(tempSize):
                        Label(tempWin,text=str(sat[i]["PRN"]),width=8).grid(column=0,row=i+1)
                        Label(tempWin,text=str(sat[i]["az"]),width=7).grid(column=1,row=i+1)
                        Label(tempWin,text=str(sat[i]["el"]),width=10).grid(column=2,row=i+1)
                        Label(tempWin,text=str(sat[i]["ss"]),width=11).grid(column=3,row=i+1)
                        Label(tempWin,text=str(sat[i]["used"]),width=6).grid(column=4,row=i+1)
        except:
                if SELF.pyVersion == '2.7.9':
                        tkMessageBox.showerror("DATA ERROR", "Will close window, try again")
                else:
                        tkinter.messagebox.showerror("DATA ERROR", "Will close window, try again")
```

```python
            tempWin.destroy()


def calDist():
    try:
        vF=SELF.vFr.get()               #get Radiobox From selection
        vT=SELF.vTo.get()               #get Radiobox To selection
    except:
        if SELF.pyVersion == '2.7.9':
            tkMessageBox.showerror("ERROR", "You need to select To and From")
            return
        else:
            tkinter.messagebox.showerror("ERROR", "You need to select To and From")
            return
#From Coordinates
    if vF==0:
        Lat1= SELF.lat              #current position of GPS
        Lon1= SELF.lon
    else:
        temp = SELF.rows[vF]["Lat"]
        Lat1 = float(temp)
        temp = SELF.rows[vF]["Lon"]
        Lon1 = float(temp)


#To Coordinates
    if vT==99:          #custom to coordinates
        Lat2 = SELF.ToLat
        Lon2 = SELF.ToLon
    else:
        temp = SELF.rows[vT]["Lat"]
        Lat2 = float(temp)
        temp = SELF.rows[vT]["Lon"]
        Lon2 = float(temp)


# Calculate the great circle distance between two points specified in decimal
# degrees. Convert decimal degrees to radians. Then use haversine formula to
# get distance in km.
    Lat1 = radians(Lat1)            #convert to radians
    Lon1 = radians(Lon1)
    Lat2 = radians(Lat2)
    Lon2 = radians(Lon2)
    dlat = Lat2 - Lat1              #calculate difference
```

```python
        dlon = Lon2 - Lon1
        #two more steps for the haversine formula
        a = sin(dlat/2)**2 + cos(Lat1) * cos(Lat2) * sin(dlon/2)**2
        SELF.calDist = 2 * asin(sqrt(a))*6371.393   #earth's radius mile 3,959
        displayDistance()

def customCoord():
        cTOP = Toplevel()
        cTOP.title( "From GPS to Custom Coords" )
        cTOP.geometry( "380x150+540+30" )#width, height, placement on x&y axis
        Label(cTOP,text='Enter Decimal Exp. 40.458321').grid(column=0,
                columnspan=2,row=0)

        Label(cTOP,text="To Latitude").grid(column=0, row=3,sticky=(W))
        SELF.vLat2=DoubleVar()
        e2=Entry(cTOP, textvariable=SELF.vLat2)
        e2.grid(column=1, row=3)
        e2.delete(0,END)
        e2.focus()

        Label(cTOP,text="To Longitude").grid(column=0, row=4,sticky=(W))
        SELF.vLon2=DoubleVar()
        e3=Entry(cTOP, textvariable=SELF.vLon2)
        e3.grid(column=1, row=4)
        e3.delete(0,END)

        Button(cTOP, text="CANCEL/Close",
                command=cTOP.destroy).grid(column=0,row=7)
        Button(cTOP, text="Calculate Distance",command=calCustDist).grid(column=1,
                row=7)

def calCustDist():
        SELF.vFr.set(0)            #this is GPS location
        SELF.vTo.set(99)  #for to coordinates entered
        try:
                SELF.ToLat=float(SELF.vLat2.get())
                SELF.ToLon=float(SELF.vLon2.get())
        except:
                if SELF.pyVersion == '2.7.9':
                        tkMessageBox.showerror("ERROR", 'Enter in Decimal Format')
                        return
                else:
```

```python
                    tkinter.messagebox.showerror("ERROR", 'Enter in Decimal Format')
                    return
        calDist()

def buttonSection():
        bFr = Frame(SELF.TOP)
        bFr.grid(column=0, row=0, sticky=(N,W,S))

        SELF.gpsControl=StringVar()
        SELF.gpsControl.set("Run  GPS")

        Button(bFr,textvariable=SELF.gpsControl, fg='green',
                command=callStartGPS).grid(column=0,row=0,sticky=(E,W))
        Button(bFr,text="EXIT", fg='red', command=callEXIT).grid(column=1,
                row=0,sticky=(E,W))
        Button(bFr,text="Satelites", fg='blue', command=callSAT).grid(column=0,
                row=1,sticky=(E,W))
        Button(bFr,text="Sat Positions", fg='blue',
                command=callSATpos).grid(column=1, row=1,sticky=(E,W))
        Button(bFr,text="Planetarium", fg='blue',
                command=callPlanetarium).grid(column=0, row=2,sticky=(E,W))
        Button(bFr,text="ISS Observation", fg='blue',
                command=callISSobservation).grid(column=1, row=2,sticky=(E,W))
        Button(bFr,text="Planets", fg='blue',
                command=callPlanets).grid(column=0,       row=3,sticky=(E,W))
        Button(bFr,text="GPS Error & More", fg='green',
                command=callErrMore).grid(column=1, row=3,sticky=(E,W))
def callErrMore():
        tempWin= Toplevel()
        tempWin.title("GPS Error and More")
        tempWin.geometry( "470x300+540+30" ) #width, height, place on x y axis
        Label(tempWin,text="Time Error % Seconds",
                width=24).grid(column=0,row=0,stick=W)
        Label(tempWin,textvariable=DISP.timeErr,width=5).grid(column=1,row=0)
        Label(tempWin,text="Longitude Error Meters",width=24).grid(column=0,row=1)
        Label(tempWin,textvariable=DISP.LongErr,width=5).grid(column=1,row=1)
        Label(tempWin,text="Latitude Error Meters",width=24).grid(column=0,row=2)
        Label(tempWin,textvariable=DISP.LatErr,width=5).grid(column=1,row=2)
        Label(tempWin,text="Vertical Error Meters",width =24).grid(column=0,row=3)
        Label(tempWin,textvariable=DISP.VertErr,width=5).grid(column=1,row=3)
        Label(tempWin,text="Climb Rate meters/second",
                width =24).grid(column=0,row=4)
```

```python
        Label(tempWin,textvariable=DISP.climb,width=5).grid(column=1,row=4)
        Label(tempWin,text="Track % from North",width =24).grid(column=0,row=5)
        Label(tempWin,textvariable=DISP.track,width=5).grid(column=1,row=5)
        Label(tempWin,text="Direction Error%",width =24).grid(column=0,row=6)
        Label(tempWin,textvariable=DISP.DirErr,width=5).grid(column=1,row=6)
        Label(tempWin,text="Speed Error Meters/Second",
                width =24).grid(column=0,row=7)
        Label(tempWin,textvariable=DISP.SpeedErr,width=5).grid(column=1,row=7)
        Label(tempWin,text="Climb Error Meters/Second",
                width =24).grid(column=0,row=8)
        Label(tempWin,textvariable=DISP.ClimbErr,width=5).grid(column=1,row=8)
        Button(tempWin,text="CLOSE",command=tempWin.destroy).grid(column=0,row=14)


def callSATpos():
        url = 'http://www.nstb.tc.faa.gov/FULL_WaasSatelliteStatus.htm'
        webbrowser.open(url)
def callPlanetarium():
        url = 'http://www.in-the-sky.org/skymap.php'
        webbrowser.open(url)
def callISSobservation():
        url = 'http://iss.astroviewer.net/observation.php'
        webbrowser.open(url)
def callPlanets():
        url = 'http://theskylive.com/planets'
        webbrowser.open(url)


def radioButton():
        lFr = LabelFrame(SELF.TOP)
        lFr.grid(column=4, row=0,rowspan=3,    sticky=(N,W,S))

        sFr = LabelFrame(lFr, text='From',width=100, height=30)
        sFr.grid(column=0, row=0,sticky=(N,W,S))
        sTo=LabelFrame(lFr, text='To',width=100, height=15)
        sTo.grid(column=1, row=0,sticky=(N,W,S))
        Button(lFr,text="Cal Distance",fg='blue',
                command=calDist).grid(column=0,row=1,sticky=W)
        Button(lFr,text="Custom To Coord",fg='white',
                command=customCoord).grid(column=1,row=1,sticky=(E,W))
#From Location
        SELF.vFr = IntVar()
        SELF.vFr.set(' ')
```

```
        Radiobutton(sFr,text=SELF.rows[0]["name"],variable=SELF.vFr,
                value=0).grid(column=3, row=0,sticky=(W))
        Radiobutton(sFr,text=SELF.rows[1]["name"],variable=SELF.vFr,
                value=1).grid(column=3, row=1, sticky=(W))
        Radiobutton(sFr,text=SELF.rows[2]["name"],variable=SELF.vFr,
                value=2).grid(column=3, row=2, sticky=(W))
        Radiobutton(sFr,text=SELF.rows[3]["name"],variable=SELF.vFr,
                value=3).grid(column=3, row=3, sticky=(W))
        Radiobutton(sFr,text=SELF.rows[4]["name"],variable=SELF.vFr,
                value=4).grid(column=3, row=4, sticky=(W))
        Radiobutton(sFr,text=SELF.rows[5]["name"],variable=SELF.vFr,
                value=5).grid(column=3,row=5, sticky=(W))
        Radiobutton(sFr,text=SELF.rows[6]["name"],variable=SELF.vFr,
                value=6).grid(column=3,row=6, sticky=(W))
# To Location
        SELF.vTo= IntVar()
        SELF.vTo.set(' ')
        Radiobutton(sTo,text=SELF.rows[1]["name"],variable=SELF.vTo,
                value=1).grid(column=3, row=0, sticky=(W))
        Radiobutton(sTo,text=SELF.rows[2]["name"],variable=SELF.vTo,
                value=2).grid(column=3, row=1, sticky=(W))
        Radiobutton(sTo,text=SELF.rows[3]["name"],variable=SELF.vTo,
                value=3).grid(column=3, row=2, sticky=(W))
        Radiobutton(sTo,text=SELF.rows[4]["name"],variable=SELF.vTo,
                value=4).grid(column=3, row=3, sticky=(W))
        Radiobutton(sTo,text=SELF.rows[5]["name"],variable=SELF.vTo,
                value=5).grid(column=3, row=4, sticky=(W))
        Radiobutton(sTo,text=SELF.rows[6]["name"],variable=SELF.vTo,
                value=6).grid(column=3, row=5, sticky=(W))
        Radiobutton(sTo,text=SELF.rows[7]["name"],variable=SELF.vTo,
                value=7).grid(column=3, row=6, sticky=(W))

def callStartGPS():
        if SELF.gpsControl.get() == "Run  GPS":
                SELF.gpsControl.set("STOP GPS")
                # this only stops display.  To stop gps run the following from the
                # command line    sudo killall gpsd
                # if you run it twice should get message "gpsd: no process found"
        else:
                SELF.gpsControl.set("Run  GPS")

def setupGPS():
```

```python
        try:
            subprocess.call(['/usr/bin/sudo','/home/pi/GPSbook/StartGPS'])
            sleep(1)
            SELF.gps_socket = agps3.GPSDSocket()
            SELF.data_stream = agps3.DataStream()
            SELF.gps_socket.connect()
            SELF.gps_socket.watch()
#initiate values as object not always available
            SELF.altM = 0
            SELF.altF = 0
            SELF.lat = 0
            SELF.lon = 0
            SELF.speedKPH = 0
            SELF.speedMPH = 0
            SELF.mode = 3
            DISP.timeErr = StringVar()
            DISP.timeErr.set(0)
            DISP.LongErr = StringVar()
            DISP.LongErr.set(0)
            DISP.LatErr = StringVar()
            DISP.LatErr.set(0)
            DISP.VertErr = StringVar()
            DISP.VertErr.set(0)
            DISP.climb = StringVar()
            DISP.climb.set(0)
            DISP.track = StringVar()
            DISP.track.set(0)
            DISP.DirErr = StringVar()
            DISP.DirErr.set(0)
            DISP.SpeedErr = StringVar()
            DISP.SpeedErr.set(0)
            DISP.ClimbErr = StringVar()
            DISP.ClimbErr.set(0)
            sleep(2)
        except(RuntimeError, TypeError,NameError):
            if SELF.pyVersion == '2.7.9':
                tkMessageBox.showerror("ERROR setupGPS",
                    "May Need to run  run shell manually \n sudo ./StartGPS")
                return
            else:
                tkinter.messagebox.showerror("ERROR setupGPS",
                    "May Need to run shell manually \n sudo ./StartGPS")
```

```
                    return

def displayUpdating():
        while True:
                msgFromGPS()      # refresh the display
                sleep(.1)

def myTimer():
        while True:
                runningGPS()      # get new location from GPS
        #       sleep(.1)         # runs fine with this commented out

def threadstart():
        dispTh=Thread(target=displayUpdating, name='dispMSG',args=())
        timeTh=Thread(target=myTimer, name='myStopTimer',args=())
        dispTh.setDaemon(True)#set all child threads before starting
        timeTh.setDaemon(True)        #set daemon so exit will stops threads
        try:
                dispTh.start()
                timeTh.start()
        except:
                print ('ERROR starting thread')

def callEXIT():
        try:
                SELF.TOP.destroy()      #closes all windows
        except:
                print ('error on quit')

def setupTk(frMain):
        if frMain==1:                   #program run as stand alone
                SELF.TOP = Tk()
        if frMain==0:                   #program imported & run from other Python script
                SELF.TOP = Toplevel()
        myGPSdisplay()                  #get the initial display filled in
        setupGPS()                      #setup GPS session
        sleep(2)
        radioButton()                   #setup location selection
        SELF.TOP.title( "GPS Center" )
        SELF.TOP.geometry( "510x300+40+30" ) #width,height,place on x y axis
        buttonSection()
        displayDistance()
```

```
        threadstart()

if __name__ == '__main__':
        setupTk(1)
        mainloop()   # Thank you, best of luck.
                            # See www.rymax.biz for additional materials
```

THE END OR THE BEGINNING

I hope that you have learned a lot and had some fun.

Visit the web site www.rymax.biz for additional information. If you wish to purchase the electronic or digital software go to my website and click on the link to FastSpring. Use the discount code "HERB SAYS THANKS". The software for this book will be listed under the same title as the book. This is a limited time special discount.

APPENDIX

Hardware and Operating Systems used

The Raspberry Pi 3 is running Raspbian GNU/Linux 8, (jessie)
Microsoft Windows 10 on a Dell PC with -Core i5-4460 CPU @3.20GHz.64 bit OS
Ubuntu 16.04 LTS on an old PC with an Intel(R) Pentium(R) 4 CPU 3.00GHz. OS 32-bit
My home network utilizes a Netgear router.

Summary for Raspberry Pi Setup

There is a good chance that the steps taken to setup your Raspberry Pi will evolve over time. The following is just a guide as to the steps that I took. While I did build a new OS for this book, you need to expect things to change, and of course I may have forgotten something, but I don't think so. Check out the web for the latest instructions.

Raspberry Pi 3   building the SD card on a Windows 10 PC
　　　I have settled on the Raspbian OS (Jessie) download site below
　　　https://www.raspberrypi.org/downloads/

　　　You will probably need to unzip, I use 7 zip, a free download   www.7-zip-org

　　　For your SD card a mimimum of 8Gb and a fast SD is recommended

　　　After unzipped I used Win32 Disk Imager to install the OS img file on to the SD card
　　　Disk Image Win32
　　　download from
　　　http://sourceforge.net/projects/win32diskimager/

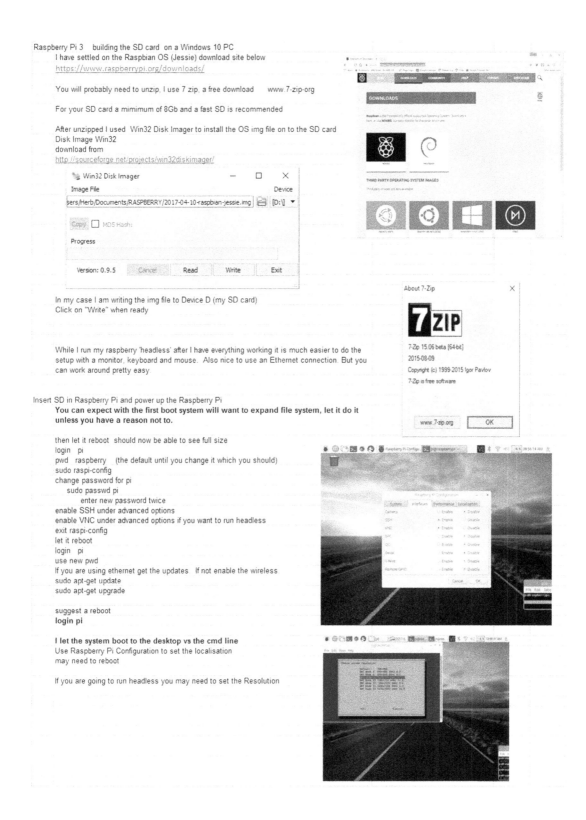

　　　In my case I am writing the img file to Device D (my SD card)
　　　Click on "Write" when ready

　　　While I run my raspberry 'headless' after I have everything working it is much easier to do the
　　　setup with a monitor, keyboard and mouse. Also nice to use an Ethernet connection. But you
　　　can work around pretty easy.

Insert SD in Raspberry Pi and power up the Raspberry Pi
　　　**You can expect with the first boot system will want to expand file system, let it do it
　　　unless you have a reason not to.**

　　　then let it reboot should now be able to see full size
　　　login   pi
　　　pwd   raspberry   (the default until you change it which you should)
　　　sudo raspi-config
　　　change password for pi
　　　　　sudo passwd pi
　　　　　　　enter new password twice
　　　enable SSH under advanced options
　　　enable VNC under advanced options if you want to run headless
　　　exit raspi-config
　　　let it reboot
　　　login   pi
　　　use new pwd
　　　If you are using ethernet get the updates   If not enable the wireless
　　　sudo apt-get update
　　　sudo apt-get upgrade

　　　suggest a reboot
　　　login pi

　　　I let the system boot to the desktop vs the cmd line
　　　Use Raspberry Pi Configuration to set the localisation
　　　may need to reboot

　　　If you are going to run headless you may need to set the Resolution

VNC install on Windows 10

Go to web site REAL VNC https://www.realvnc.com/download/viewer/windows/ and click on Download
VNC Viewer 6.1.0 in my case. This will download an executable program that you can then copy to your
desktop if desired. You will need your Raspberry Pi 's IP address to login. Your should be able to obtain this
from your router, or the command "ifconfig" on the Raspberry.

logging on to the Pi from Windows Direct Connection via Ether-Net

You need to have installed VNC Viewer on the PC. Connect the PC and the Raspberry Pi using a standard ether net cable. (You don't need a cross over connection.) The hardest thing is to figure out the ip address of the Raspberry. To find it I ran 'ifconfig' on the Raspberry. Use your console or other connection if possible.

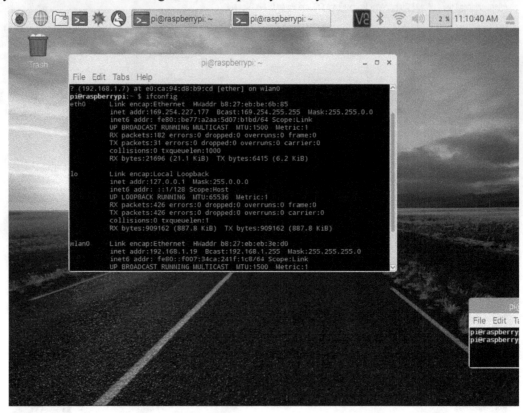

My connection IP address is 169.254.227.177 as shown above under "eth0". Log in as pi, and all should work as well as over the router.

logging on to the Pi from Ubuntu-Linux via Router or Wireless

There are a lot of ways to do this, the simplest method I have found is to use VNC. You must have VNC enabled on the Pi good idea to have SSH enabled also. You probably have already set these.

Download the VNC Viewer software from REALVNC https://www.realvnc.com/download/viewer/linux/

Determine the Raspberry Pi address on the router with ifconfig or via your router.

Start the VNC Viewer and enter the address.

I get an RSA warning, no, not from NSA. Just accept and you will not get the warning the next time. Now that you are logged on to the Raspberry Pi.

logging on to the Pi from Ubuntu-Linux Direct Connection via Ether-Net

You need to have VNC Viewer installed on the Ubuntu. You do not need a cross over ether net cable. One of the best sources I have found is "Mihaly's projects http://www.muonhunter.com/blog/direct-ethernet-connection-to-a-raspberry-pi-under-ubuntu. I have summarized with some screen shots.

You will need to make some changes on the Ubuntu. Add a connection and edit the connection.

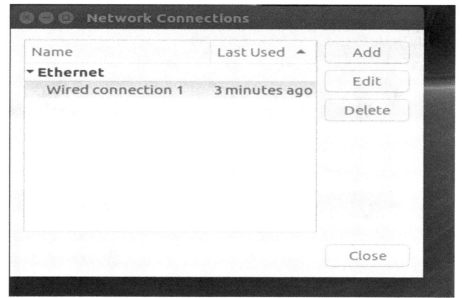

You will also need to edit the settings.

Connect the ether net cable. Wait a short period and from the command prompt on the Ubuntu enter the following: cat /var/lib/misc/dnsmasq.leases this should give you the address you need.

Run VNC Viewer with the address. 10.42.0.248   My viewer exhibit shows the router and the direct connect address.

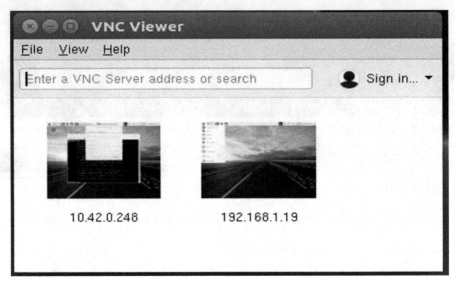

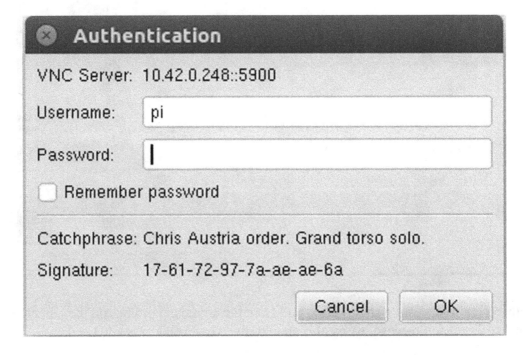

You can also easily get to a Raspberry command prompt by running ssh from the command prompt on Ubuntu.

From a terminal prompt on Ubuntu enter the command "ssh -X pi@10.42.0.248". Use a capital X (with your IP address). You will be asked for the pi password.

```
herb@UbuntoDell: ~
File Edit View Search Terminal Help
herb@UbuntoDell:~$ cat /var/lib/misc/dnsmasq.leases
1494006221 b8:27:eb:be:6b:85 10.42.0.248 raspberrypi 01:b8:27:eb:be:6b:85
herb@UbuntoDell:~$ ssh -X pi@10.42.0.248
The authenticity of host '10.42.0.248 (10.42.0.248)' can't be established.
ECDSA key fingerprint is SHA256:aS2xYAN0r3JSt9ISv9l5Q9kwpjllIpzyKuVkkWxMZGw.
Are you sure you want to continue connecting (yes/no)?
```

```
pi@raspberrypi: ~
File Edit View Search Terminal Help
individual files in /usr/share/doc/*/copyright.

Debian GNU/Linux comes with ABSOLUTELY NO WARRANTY, to the extent
permitted by applicable law.
Last login: Thu May  4 13:55:47 2017
pi@raspberrypi:~ $
```

Battery or Auxiliary Power

If you are just running the Pi and the GPS your power requirements are minimal. You need 5V DC, but it terms of milliamps the power needed falls off dramatically with a bare bones system. While there are many choices I am just going to cover a few options. Consider that if you input power through the standard Pi input there is a voltage regulator built in to the Pi. Another option is to bring power in via the 5V pin, but beware there is no voltage protection built in with this method. For my robots I have experimented with building battery packs and using the 5V pin and of course external voltage regulators. While it worked, I don't recommend the home built approach unless you are going to get into efficient voltage regulators. I recommend that you go with one of the battery devices somewhat designed for the intended purpose, powering the Pi. I have been very happy with the USB Battery Pack for Raspberry Pi – 10000mAh, PID 1566 from Adafruit. Cost $49.95. (Note, there is now a newer version same PID, cost $39.95, I have not tried the newer version.) If you are running the GPS while in your car, you can get an adapter that plugs into the cigarette lighter. Check the voltage for 5V, testing is always good. You can also power the Pi from the USB port of your computer. As you determine your needs I am sure you will be able to find a suitable option.

PuTTY for Windows

For our communications you will NOT need PuTTY© installed on your PC, but it is a very useful program. The following describes how to obtain the PuTTY executable. Go to the main PuTTY Download Page. http://www.chiark.greenend.org.uk/~sgtatham/putty/download.html. From this page you can select the appropriate file. I suggest you get the Windows installer for everything except PuTTYtel. At this point the latest release is version .63.

Open PuTTY and click on SSH, make appropriate changes. For Host Name or IP address I am using the IP address (for the Pi) and Port 22. Under Category select (Connection SSH X11) and if you need it Enable X11 forwarding. Under Category Session you can name your file under Saved Sessions, which is a real good idea. There are lots of options you can set, but we are just using PuTTY to gain command level access to the Raspberry. The PuTTY help files should have been included if things are not working.

If you need X11 forwarding.

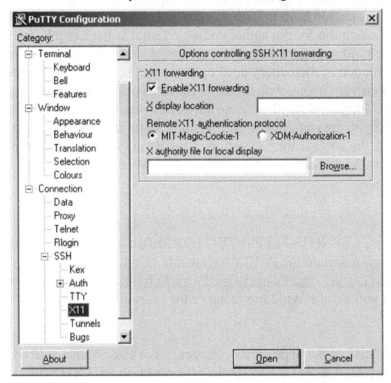

PuTTY for Linux

The install is very straight forward. Just run "sudo apt-get install putty". The PuTTY settings are the same as for the Windows version mentioned above. Nice to have but not needed as we will use the standard ssh included with Ubuntu-Linux.

Geany for Windows

The program has many useful features as well as being a very nice text editor. Go to www.geany.org . The geany-1.2.3.1 setup.exe Full Installer is approximately 8Mb.

Geany for Raspberry Pi

On the Raspberry raspbian jessie OS Geany is already installed. If you need to install it is pretty straight forward enter: "sudo apt-get install geany". If you want to install on the Ubuntu the same command works.

Linux Shell Scripts

A few hints for making your scripts executable. Not your Python scripts, Python handles that. You can write your script using any text editor, vi or vim, Geany, nano, etc.

- The file name doesn't need an extension.

- Comments are a line starting with a pound sign '#'

- You need to have permission to execute or run the script. After you have saved your script open a terminal window and go to the directory where you saved the script. Type 'ls -l filename' for example. (small letter 'L') The permissions will be shown. Something similar to the following table, third row.

position 1	2	3	4	5	6	7	8	9	10
directory flag	User read	User write	User execute	Group read	Group write	Group execute	Other read	Other write	Other execute
-	r	w	-	r	-	-	r	-	-
-	r	w	x	r	-	-	r	-	-

You need to make the script an executable. You can do this from a terminal window. Be in the directory with your script and type chmod u+x filename. Then retype the ls -l filename and you should see the change as shown on row 4 of the preceding table. (NOTE a small letter L) To run the script from the terminal window, be in the same directory and type. ./filename or type . filename (Notice the . and space) What our StartGPS file looks like.

Linux Commands

Before using understand that many of the commands have options that are not shown here. For those who may have forgotten some simple Linux commands, a very quick refresher course follows. This is only the tip of the iceberg, just listing a few. Before we go any further, a few quick words on commands. They can do damage, they are not very user friendly; they will destroy without asking twice. So make sure the command you enter is the command that you want and that you know what the command is going to do. Remember when you execute a command that involves a filename you may want to proceed the filename with a "./". Example "cat ./filename".

cat filname	list contents of file
cat filename > filename2	copy filename to filename2
cat /etc/debian_version	this will show what version of Debian you are running
cat /etc/os-release	will show misc. os information
cat /etc/issue	Show OS version
cd	change to home directory
cd /	change to root directory
cd ..	move up one level in the directory tree
chgrp newgroup filename	change the group name for the named file
chown newower filename	change the owner of filename to the new owner name
chmod u+x filename	add permission for user to execute filename
clear	clear the screen can also use Ctrl L

cp filename filename2	copy filename to filname2
date	show current day, date and time
df -h	File systems mounted, size, used, avail Use%, where mounted
df -k	File system as above, but include 1K-Blocks
dmesg	This will show the devices attached, very useful for finding PL2303 and other serial devices attached
echo $SHELL	to see what shell you are running
echo $PATH	shows current search path
fclist	List fonts on system
find -name filename	find the specified filename
find -i name filename	Find the specified filename, ignore case
free -m	display memory used and free
hostname -I	show system current host name
id	what user you are and what groups you are in
ifconfig	display connections information, (eth0, lo, wlan0, etc)
ifconfig -a	show all connections information, mac address next to HWaddr
ip addr show	show connection addresses
kill number	If you need to stop a runaway process, number is the process ID (PID)
lp filename	print filename to default printer
lpstat -t	show default printer
ls	displays current directory
ls -l	displays current directory with permissions (note small Ls)
ls - u -l filename	List last access time
lsmod	List module Size and Used by
lsusb	list usb devices running on computer
lsusb -v	run as sudo for a complete list, with v is a verbose list
mkdir filename	make a new directory
more filename	list the file, will do in pages
mv filename filname2	move or rename filename to filname2
pwd	to see what your current directory is
ps –help all	Help information for process's (NOTE there are two '-'
ps -p$$	displays what shell you are running
ps -T or ps	show all processes on this terminal
ps -A	show all processes running on computer
ps aux	show all process running on computer, user, PID & more

pstree	show all processes in a tree format
ps -p$$	show current PID TTY TIME CMD
uname -a	display version and kernel
rm filename	delete file specified
reboot	do an immediate shutdown and then reboot
reset	use when console has character map a mess, resets to standard
rmdir directory	remove specified directory
rm -r directory	remove specified directory and contents of the directory
shutdown -h now	shutdown the computer now, you may need sudo in front of command
tail -n 10 /var/log/syslog	View last 10 entries in syslog
who	list all users
whoami	to see what user you are

GPS setup for Travel

The Raspberry using the battery pack and running with a direct ether-net connection to the Windows Laptop.

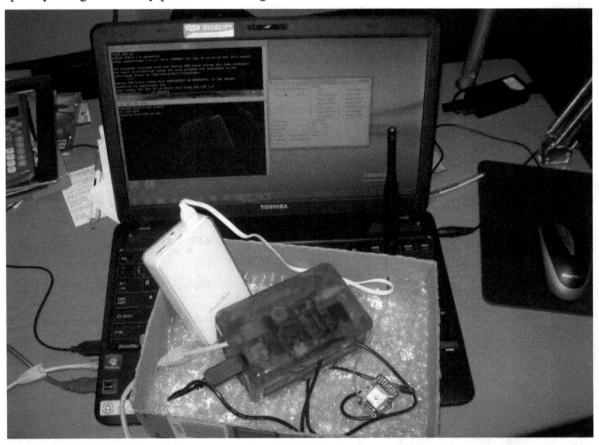

Reference Sites

Raspberry

http://www.raspberrypi.org

http://www.engadget.com/2012/09/05/cambridge-university-raspberry-pi-guide/

http://www.engadget.com/2012/09/04/raspberry-pi-getting-started-guide-how-to/

http://www.raspberrypi.org/downloads

http://elinux.org/R-Pi_Troubleshooting

http://elinux.org/RPi_Hardware#Power

http://shallowsky.com/blog/hardware/pi-battery.html

http://elinux.org/RPi_raspi-config

Raspberry – GPS

https://learn.adafruit.com/adafruit-ultimate-gps-on-the-raspberry-pi/setting-everything-up?view=all

https://en.wikipedia.org/wiki/Latitude

http://en.wikipedia.org/wiki/Haversine_formula

http://www.offroaders.com/info/tech-corner/reading/GPS-Coordinates.htm

http://www.movable-type.co.uk/scripts/latlong.html

http://www.gpsvisualizer.com/calculators

http://www.earthpoint.us/convert.aspx

https://www.pinterest.com/kmcdavid/social-studies-latitude-and-longitude/

https://en.wikipedia.org/wiki/Latitude

https://upload.wikimedia.org/wikipedia/commons/5/53/MercNormSph_enhanced.png

Python

https://pypi.python.org/pypi/gps3/

http://www.catb.org/gpsd/gpsd_json.html

www.astro.ufl.edu

www.sthurlow.com

www.learnpython.org

http://www.astro.ufl.edu/~warner/prog/python.html

www.tutorialspoint.com/python/index.htm

https://developers.google.com/edu/python

http://www.python.org/dev/peps/pep-0008/

http://docs.python.org/2/library/subprocess.html

http://docs.python.org/2/library/stdtypes.html

http://mkaz.com/solog/python-string-format

http://www.tutorialspoint.com/python/python_strings.htm

http://docs.python.org/2/library/string.html

Tkinter

http://effbot.org/tkinterbook/grid.htm

http://infohost.nmt.edu/tcc/help/pubs/tkinter/web/index.html

http://www.tkdocs.com/tutorial/windows.html

http://effbot.org/tkinterbook/

http://www.tutorialspoint.com/python/python_gui_programming.htm

http://www.tutorialspoint.com/python/tk_messagebox.htm

Windows

https://www.realvnc.com/download/viewer/windows/

Linux

https://www.realvnc.com/download/viewer/linux/

http://steve-parker.org/sh/intro.shtml

http://linuxtutorial.info/modules.php?name=MContent&pageid=329

Direct Connect Ether-net

http://www.muonhunter.com/blog/direct-ethernet-connection-to-a-raspberry-pi-under-ubuntu

http://pihw.wordpress.com/guides/direct-network-connection/

PuTTY

http://www.chiark.greenend.org.uk/~sgtatham/putty/download.html

Geany

www.geany.org

www.ingramcontent.com/pod-product-compliance
Lightning Source LLC
Chambersburg PA
CBHW060443060326
40690CB00019B/4308